Music
Through Time
CLARINET BOOK 4

SELECTED AND
EDITED BY

Paul Harris

MUSIC DEPARTMENT

OXFORD
UNIVERSITY PRESS

OXFORD
UNIVERSITY PRESS

Great Clarendon Street, Oxford OX2 6DP, England
198 Madison Avenue, New York, NY 10016, USA

Oxford University Press is a department of the University of Oxford.
It furthers the University's aim of excellence in research, scholarship,
and education by publishing worldwide

7 9 10 8 6

ISBN 978-0-19-335686-3

Music and text origination by
Enigma Music Production Services, Amersham, Bucks.
Printed in Great Britain on acid-free paper by
Halstan & Co. Ltd., Amersham, Bucks.

All of the pieces in this collection are arranged
for clarinet and piano by Paul Harris

CONTENTS

1645
Coranto

Bulstrode Whitelocke
(1605–1675)

The famous Scottish pirate, Captain William Kidd, was born. Legend says he buried a vast treasure and that people have been searching for it ever since. In the same century King Charles I was executed and Oliver Cromwell established as Lord Protector of England.

Bulstrode Whitelocke, an MP during the time of Oliver Cromwell, is thought to have written this short piece as proof that he understood the art of making music. The coranto is a typical dance of the period, performed with fast running and jumping steps broken up by hops between the steps.

* Try adding the second trill key to the C fingering for the Ds in this bar.

This year marks the birth of Denis de Diderot, the famous French philosopher and encyclopaedist, and the death of Arcangelo Corelli, the great Italian composer. The first ever smallpox epidemic spread from sailors at the Cape of Good Hope, and Stradivari was making his world-famous violins.

Bach's sinfonias were written partly as studies for the progressing musician, so that, in the composer's own words, they might 'obtain a cantabile style of playing, and together with this get a strong foretaste of composition'.

1713
Sinfonia

Johann Sebastian Bach
(1685–1750)

1720
Sonata

Edmond Halley, the man who named Halley's Comet, was appointed Royal Astronomer, and Jonathan Swift began writing *Gulliver's Travels*. Daniel Defoe published *The Adventures of Robinson Crusoe*.

Scarlatti is best known for his keyboard sonatas; he wrote more than 500 over a period of 25 years. He was an accomplished harpsichord player: in a trial of skill with Handel at the palace of Cardinal Ottoboni in Rome he was judged to be the better player. It caused a great stir, but Handel was pacified as it was also judged that he was clearly a better organist!

Domenico Scarlatti
(1685–1757)

* Use first trill key (RH first finger)

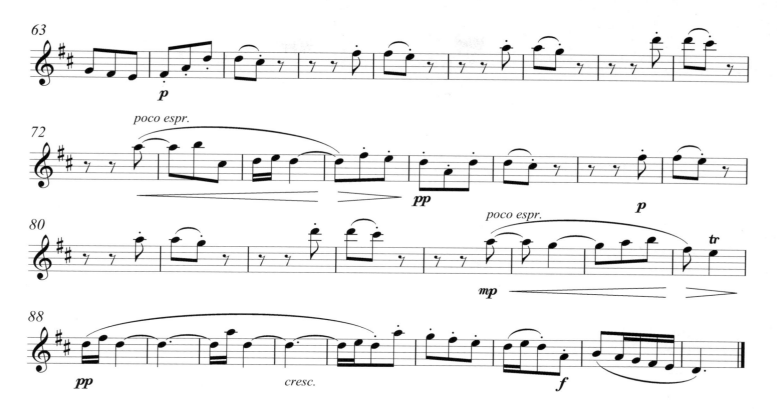

Robert Walpole, the first Prime Minister of Great Britain, died. One of the most unusually named conflicts in modern history, the War of Jenkins' Ear, a nine-year struggle with Spain, took place during his premiership.

Molter's four concertos were the first ever to be written for the clarinet. He wrote most of his music in the latter part of his life, when he was in charge of court music in Karlsruhe. The ruling Duke was so pleased with him that, as a mark of respect when he died, he left his post vacant for a whole year, despite the existence of a suitable candidate to fill it.

1745

Adagio from Concerto no. 3

Johann Melchior Molter

(1696–1765)

1772
Allegretto from Divertimento no. 2 K131

Wolfgang Amadeus Mozart
(1756–1791)

Sir William Congreve, the man who invented the first missiles ever used by the British military, was born. It was his rockets whose 'red glare' is mentioned in the American national anthem. The slave trade began to falter following a successful lawsuit brought against a slave owner by his slave in England.

Whilst on a trip to Italy in 1772, Mozart heard Gregorio Allegri's *Miserere* in performance in the Sistine Chapel. Afterwards he wrote it out in its entirety from memory, only returning to correct minor errors. He thereby produced the first illegal copy of this closely-guarded property of the Vatican! This piece, written in the same year, comes from a Divertimento for wind instruments designed for performance outdoors.

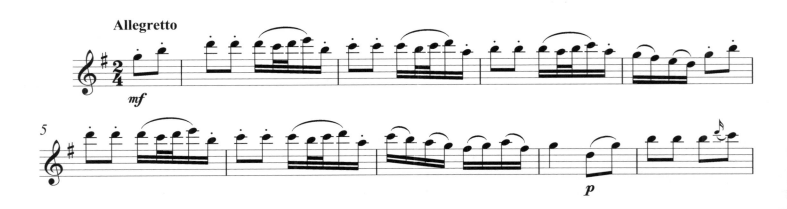

1802
Adagio from Sonata no. 7

Xavier Lefèvre
(1763–1829)

Madame Tussaud opened her famous wax-work museum in London, and Beethoven gave the first performance of his 'Moonlight' Sonata. The estimated population of the planet reached one billion.

Lefèvre was a brilliant 18th-century clarinettist, and it was his great knowledge of the instrument that allowed him to write such sympathetic music for it. He wrote a total of fifteen clarinet sonatas, more than any other composer, and is also responsible for adding the C♯/G♯ key to the standard five-key clarinet of the time.

Napoleon Bonaparte abdicated as Emperor of France and
George Stephenson designed his first locomotive. Adolphe Sax,
the inventor of the saxophone, was born in Wallonia, Belgium.

Danzi was a German cellist and composer, who knew both
Mozart and Beethoven. He composed in many different genres,
but is perhaps best known today for his wind quintets.
A pot pourri is a composition that is made up of several
pleasing tunes, also known as a fantasia.

1814
Pot Pourri

Franz Danzi
(1763–1826)

1843
Song without Words, op. 67, no. 2

Felix Mendelssohn

(1809–1847)

The first tunnel under the Thames was completed by Isambard Kingdom Brunel. Charles Dickens published his novel, *A Christmas Carol*. Queen Victoria proclaimed Hong Kong to be a British colony.

Mendelssohn was thought to be the most prodigious child talent after Mozart, giving his first public performance at the age of nine. In spite of early fame, he strove to lead a normal life, and was wary of what he considered to be the outlandish innovation by some of his contemporaries, such as Liszt. The *Songs without Words* are perhaps his most famous piano works.

OXFORD

Music Through Time

CLARINET BOOK 4
PIANO ACCOMPANIMENTS

CONTENTS

SELECTED AND EDITED BY
Paul Harris

1645
Coranto

Bulstrode Whitelocke

(1605–1675)

The famous Scottish pirate, Captain William Kidd, was born. Legend says he buried a vast treasure and that people have been searching for it ever since. In the same century King Charles I was executed and Oliver Cromwell established as Lord Protector of England.

Bulstrode Whitelocke, an MP during the time of Oliver Cromwell, is thought to have written this short piece as proof that he understood the art of making music. The coranto is a typical dance of the period, performed with fast running and jumping steps broken up by hops between the steps.

* Try adding the second trill key to the C fingering for the Ds in this bar.

1713
Sinfonia

Johann Sebastian Bach
(1685–1750)

This year marks the birth of Denis de Diderot, the famous French philosopher and encyclopaedist, and the death of Arcangelo Corelli, the great Italian composer. The first ever smallpox epidemic spread from sailors at the Cape of Good Hope, and Stradivari was making his world-famous violins.

Bach's sinfonias were written partly as studies for the progressing musician, so that, in the composer's own words, they might 'obtain a cantabile style of playing, and together with this get a strong foretaste of composition'.

1720
Sonata

Domenico Scarlatti
(1685–1757)

Edmond Halley, the man who named Halley's Comet, was appointed Royal Astronomer, and Jonathan Swift began writing *Gulliver's Travels*. Daniel Defoe published *The Adventures of Robinson Crusoe*.

Scarlatti is best known for his keyboard sonatas; he wrote more than 500 over a period of 25 years. He was an accomplished harpsichord player: in a trial of skill with Handel at the palace of Cardinal Ottoboni in Rome he was judged to be the better player. It caused a great stir, but Handel was pacified as it was also judged that he was clearly a better organist!

Non presto, ma a tempo di ballo

* Use first trill key (RH first finger)

Adagio from Concerto no. 3

Johann Melchior Molter
(1696–1765)

Robert Walpole, the first Prime Minister of Great Britain, died. One of the most unusually named conflicts in modern history, the War of Jenkins' Ear, a nine-year struggle with Spain, took place during his premiership.

Molter's four concertos were the first ever to be written for the clarinet. He wrote most of his music in the latter part of his life, when he was in charge of court music in Karlsruhe. The ruling Duke was so pleased with him that, as a mark of respect when he died, he left his post vacant for a whole year, despite the existence of a suitable candidate to fill it.

1772
Allegretto from
Divertimento no. 2 K131

Wolfgang Amadeus Mozart
(1756–1791)

Sir William Congreve, the man who invented the first missiles ever used by the British military, was born. It was his rockets whose 'red glare' is mentioned in the American national anthem. The slave trade began to falter following a successful lawsuit brought against a slave owner by his slave in England.

Whilst on a trip to Italy in 1772, Mozart heard Gregorio Allegri's *Miserere* in performance in the Sistine Chapel. Afterwards he wrote it out in its entirety from memory, only returning to correct minor errors. He thereby produced the first illegal copy of this closely-guarded property of the Vatican! This piece, written in the same year, comes from a Divertimento for wind instruments designed for performance outdoors.

Madame Tussaud opened her famous wax-work museum in London, and Beethoven gave the first performance of his 'Moonlight' Sonata. The estimated population of the planet reached one billion.

Lefèvre was a brilliant 18th-century clarinettist, and it was his great knowledge of the instrument that allowed him to write such sympathetic music for it. He wrote a total of fifteen clarinet sonatas, more than any other composer, and is also responsible for adding the C♯/G♯ key to the standard five-key clarinet of the time.

Adagio from Sonata no. 7

Xavier Lefèvre
(1763–1829)

Napoleon Bonaparte abdicated as Emperor of France and
George Stephenson designed his first locomotive. Adolphe Sax,
the inventor of the saxophone, was born in Wallonia, Belgium.

Danzi was a German cellist and composer, who knew both
Mozart and Beethoven. He composed in many different genres,
but is perhaps best known today for his wind quintets.
A pot pourri is a composition that is made up of several
pleasing tunes, also known as a fantasia.

Franz Danzi
(1763–1826)

1843

Song without Words, op. 67, no. 2

Felix Mendelssohn

(1809–1847)

The first tunnel under the Thames was completed by Isambard Kingdom Brunel. Charles Dickens published his novel, *A Christmas Carol.* Queen Victoria proclaimed Hong Kong to be a British colony.

Mendelssohn was thought to be the most prodigious child talent after Mozart, giving his first public performance at the age of nine. In spite of early fame, he strove to lead a normal life, and was wary of what he considered to be the outlandish innovation by some of his contemporaries, such as Liszt. The *Songs without Words* are perhaps his most famous piano works.

1875
Andante

Carl Baermann
(1810–1885)

The 'All England Croquet Club' at Wimbledon was persuaded to replace a croquet lawn with a tennis court, giving rise to the eponymous grand slam tournament. Bizet's *Carmen* received its first performance in Paris.

Son of the virtuoso clarinettist Heinrich Baermann, Carl was also an excellent player in his own right. He wrote a vast amount of educational music, and one of his clarinet methods remains one of the most used even now. This romantic movement was originally, and perhaps surprisingly, written as a study.

1910
Dances from Szeged

Zoltan Vallassa
(1848–1920)

The Earth passed through the tail of Halley's Comet, which led to rumours of widespread cyanide poisoning as a result of its poisonous gases. Needless to say, this was made up by the newspapers to increase circulation! Thomas Crapper, the English inventor, died aged 64.

Vallassa's *Dances from Szeged* are based on the traditional Hungarian folk dances from the great plain of Alföld, which covers more than half of the country. The native dances are lively and fun, yet their harmonies evoke the bleak landscape in which they were conceived.

Elizabeth Alexandra Mary Windsor was born; she later became Her Majesty Queen Elizabeth II, one of the longest serving monarchs in British history. John Logie Baird demonstrated a mechanical moving image system, a precursor of television. The UK went on a 'General Strike'.

Walton wrote this musical accompaniment to Edith Sitwell's *Façade* poems in the attic of the Sitwells' house, as he did most of his compositions in the 1920s. This piece led to him being branded an avant-garde modernist, and dealt him a rather notorious reputation. Nevertheless, *Façade* has become one of his most enduringly popular works.

William Walton
(1902–1983)

1936
Christmas Dance

Ralph Vaughan Williams
(1872–1958)

King Edward VIII abdicated in order to be allowed to marry the American divorcee Mrs Simpson. Ralph Neves, an American jockey, was killed during a race at the Bay Meadows Racetrack in California; he was later seen dashing down to the jockey rooms to dress for the last race, having 'woken up' on a slab in the morgue with his toe already tagged!

Vaughan Williams was much influenced by the melodies and rhythms of Tudor music, some of which can be found in this piece, an arrangement of a movement from his Suite for Viola and Orchestra.

The first British mobile phone call was made. Mikhail Gorbachev became leader of the Soviet Union. The Russian-born painter Marc Chagall and the famous actor and film director Orson Welles died.

John Rutter is one of Britain's most popular composers. His style is highly melodic and approachable. He has written countless carols and other choral works, as well as music for television. The serene and haunting *Pie Jesu* is the third movement of his *Requiem*.

Fantastical Micro-variations on a theme by Mozart

2006 celebrates the 250th birthday of Wolfgang Amadeus Mozart, arguably the greatest composer that has ever lived. In 1791, the year of his death, he wrote a clarinet concerto for his friend Anton Stadler. It remains the finest concerto ever written for the instrument. Here are some tiny variations based on the main theme from the first movement. Mozart was a great practical joker, so he would probably have loved the jokes contained within.

Paul Harris
(b. 1957)

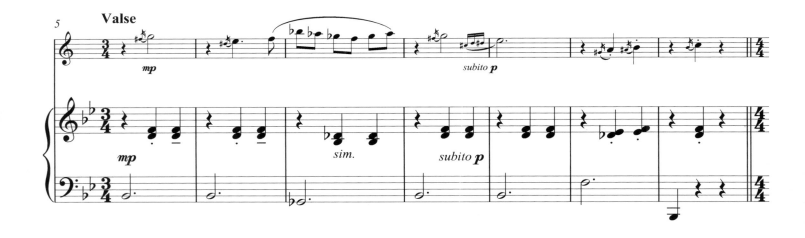

1875
Andante

Carl Baermann
(1810–1885)

The 'All England Croquet Club' at Wimbledon was persuaded to replace a croquet lawn with a tennis court, giving rise to the eponymous grand slam tournament. Bizet's *Carmen* received its first performance in Paris.

Son of the virtuoso clarinettist Heinrich Baermann, Carl was also an excellent player in his own right. He wrote a vast amount of educational music, and one of his clarinet methods remains one of the most used even now. This romantic movement was originally, and perhaps surprisingly, written as a study.

The Earth passed through the tail of Halley's Comet, which led to rumours of widespread cyanide poisoning as a result of its poisonous gases. Needless to say, this was made up by the newspapers to increase circulation! Thomas Crapper, the English inventor, died aged 64.

Vallassa's *Dances from Szeged* are based on the traditional Hungarian folk dances from the great plain of Alföld, which covers more than half of the country. The native dances are lively and fun, yet their harmonies evoke the bleak landscape in which they were conceived.

1910
Dances from Szeged

Zoltan Vallassa
(1848–1920)

Elizabeth Alexandra Mary Windsor was born; she later became Her Majesty Queen Elizabeth II, one of the longest serving monarchs in British history. John Logie Baird demonstrated a mechanical moving image system, a precursor of television. The UK went on a 'General Strike'.

Walton wrote this musical accompaniment to Edith Sitwell's *Façade* poems in the attic of the Sitwells' house, as he did most of his compositions in the 1920s. This piece led to him being branded an avant-garde modernist, and dealt him a rather notorious reputation. Nevertheless, *Façade* has become one of his most enduringly popular works.

1926

Tango-Pasodoblé

William Walton
(1902–1983)

1936
Christmas Dance

Ralph Vaughan Williams
(1872–1958)

King Edward VIII abdicated in order to be allowed to marry the American divorcee Mrs Simpson. Ralph Neves, an American jockey, was killed during a race at the Bay Meadows Racetrack in California; he was later seen dashing down to the jockey rooms to dress for the last race, having 'woken up' on a slab in the morgue with his toe already tagged!

Vaughan Williams was much influenced by the melodies and rhythms of Tudor music, some of which can be found in this piece, an arrangement of a movement from his Suite for Viola and Orchestra.

1985
Pie Jesu

John Rutter
(b. 1945)

The first British mobile phone call was made. Mikhail Gorbachev became leader of the Soviet Union. The Russian-born painter Marc Chagall and the famous actor and film director Orson Welles died.

John Rutter is one of Britain's most popular composers. His style is highly melodic and approachable. He has written countless carols and other choral works, as well as music for television. The serene and haunting *Pie Jesu* is the third movement of his *Requiem*.

Fantastical Micro-variations on a theme by Mozart

Paul Harris

(b. 1957)

2006 celebrates the 250th birthday of Wolfgang Amadeus Mozart, arguably the greatest composer that has ever lived. In 1791, the year of his death, he wrote a clarinet concerto for his friend Anton Stadler. It remains the finest concerto ever written for the instrument. Here are some tiny variations based on the main theme from the first movement. Mozart was a great practical joker, so he would probably have loved the jokes contained within.